CONTENTS

Author Chris Oxlade

Is science in the playground?

Yes, it is! Lots of science happens in a playground. The playground rides could not work without science. A see-saw is a simple machine called a lever. It has a long arm and a point in the middle called a pivot. As you ride on the see-saw, the lever tips up and down on the pivot.

See-saw

Lever

Pivot

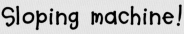

Sloping machine!

A ramp is the simplest machine of all. It is easier to walk up a ramp to the top of a hill than it is to climb a steep hillside.

What is a wheel?

A wheel is a very simple machine that can spin around. Wheels let other machines, such as skateboards, bicycles, cars and trains, roll along smoothly. They also make it easy to move heavy weights in carts and wheelbarrows.

Feel

Press the palm of your hand onto a table. A force called friction stops you sliding your hand along.

What makes things stop and start?

Pushes and pulls make things stop and start. Scientists use the word 'force' for pushes and pulls. Forces are all around us. The force of gravity pulls things downwards. It makes a rollercoaster car hurtle downhill. It also slows the car on the uphill parts of the track.

Rollercoaster

Why do fireworks flash and bang?

Fireworks flash and bang because they are full of chemicals that burn. The chemicals have lots of energy stored in them. When they burn, the energy changes to light, heat and sound. We use chemicals that burn in other places too, such as cookers, heaters and car engines.

Fireworks

How do candles burn?

Candles are made of wax and a wick (string). When the wick is lit, the wax around it melts. The wick then soaks up the liquid wax and the heat of the flame turns the wax into a gas (vapour), which burns away. As the wax becomes vapour it cools the wick, allowing the candle to burn slowly.

Hot! Hot! Hot!

The hottest-ever temperature recorded was in a science laboratory. It was four hundred million degrees Celsius (400,000,000°C).

What is a thermometer?

A thermometer tells us how hot something is. This is called temperature. The numbers written on a thermometer are normally degrees Celsius (°C). If you put a thermometer in cold water, it shows 0°C. If you put it in boiling water it shows 100°C. A thermometer can also measure your body temperature.

Remember

Which piece of equipment is used to measure how hot or cold something is?

5

What is in an electric motor?

Magnets and wires. Electricity from a battery passes through the wires. This turns the wires into a magnet. Two more magnets on each side of the motor push and pull against the wires. This makes a thin metal rod (spindle) spin around.

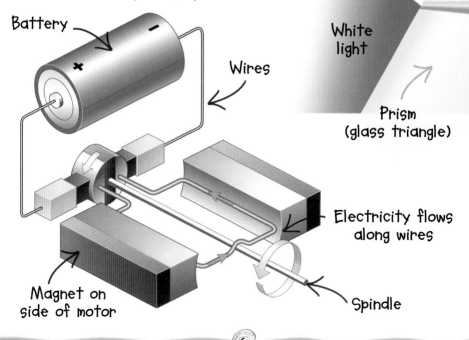

Battery

Wires

White light

Prism (glass triangle)

Electricity flows along wires

Magnet on side of motor

Spindle

Why does light bend?

Light rays travel in straight lines. When light shines through a prism, the rays bend because light travels more slowly through glass than air. Sunlight is called white light, but it is made up of a mixture of colours. When white light passes through a prism it splits into many colours, like a rainbow.

Fast as light!

Light is the fastest thing in the Universe. It travels 300,000 kilometres every second. That means it could travel around the Earth seven times in less than a second!

Rainbow colours

Make

On a sunny day, stand with your back to the Sun. Spray water into the air and you should see a rainbow!

What is the loudest sound?

The roar of a jet engine is the loudest sound we normally hear. It is thousands of times louder than someone shouting. Sounds this loud can damage our ears if we are too close to them. The quietest sounds we can hear are things like rustling leaves.

Where is science in a city?

Everywhere! In a big city, almost every machine, building and vehicle is based on science. Cars, buses and trains help us move around the city. Scientists and engineers have also worked out how to build tall skyscrapers where people live and work.

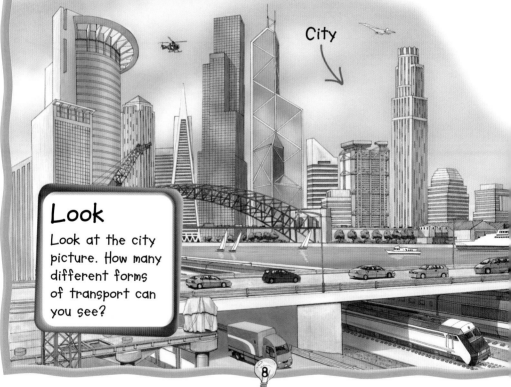

City

Look

Look at the city picture. How many different forms of transport can you see?

8

Railway signals

Who works railway signals?

Nobody does! The signals work by themselves. Electronic parts on the track work out if a train is passing. Then a computer changes the signals to red, to stop another train moving onto the same piece of track.

How do skyscrapers stay up?

Skyscrapers stay up because they have a strong frame on the inside. The frame is made from steel and concrete. These are very strong materials. Normally you can't see the frame. It is hidden by the skyscraper's walls. The walls hang on the frame.

Plane spotters!

There's science at an airport, too. A radar machine uses radio waves to find aircraft in the sky. This helps people at the airport to guide the aircraft onto the runway.

How do you make magnets?

By using another magnet! Magnets are made from lumps of iron or steel. You can turn a piece of iron into a magnet by stroking it with another magnet. A magnet can also be made by sending electricity through a coil of wire. This is called an electromagnet. Some electromagnets are so strong, they can pick up cars.

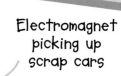

Electromagnet picking up scrap cars

VF 2314

Count

Find a magnet at home (you can use a fridge magnet). How many paper clips can your magnet pick up?

Does a magnet have a field?

Yes — but it's not a field of grass! The area around a magnet is called a magnetic field. A magnetic field is shown by drawing lines around a magnet. The Earth has a magnetic field, too. It is as though there is a giant magnet inside the Earth.

Magnetic field around the Earth

What are poles?

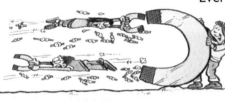

Every magnet has two poles. These are where the pull of a magnet is strongest. They are called the north pole and the south pole. A north pole and a south pole always pull towards each other. Two north poles always push each other away. So do two south poles.

Handy rock!

Some rocks act like magnets. Years ago, people used magnetic rocks to find their way. If they let the rock spin round, it always pointed in the same direction.

Where does electricity come from?

Battery

Electricity comes to your home along cables from power stations. The cables are held off the ground by pylons. Around your home are holes in the wall called sockets. When a machine is plugged into a socket, electricity flows out to work the machine.

Electric!

Our homes are full of machines that work using electricity. If there was no electricity we wouldn't have televisions, lights, washing machines or computers!

Power station

Remember

Mains electricity is very dangerous. It could kill you. Never play with mains sockets in your home.

12

Light bulb

What is a circuit?

A circuit is a loop that electricity moves around. This circuit is made up of a battery, a light bulb and a switch. If the switch is turned off, the loop would be broken. Then the electricity would stop moving and the light would go out.

Switch

When is electricity in the sky?

When there's a thunderstorm! During a storm, a kind of electricity called static electricity builds up. This can make a big flash, that lights up the sky. This is lightning. The hot lightning heats up the air around it and this makes a loud clap. This is thunder.

Pylon holds cables off the ground

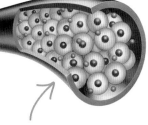

Electricity flows along the cables

What waves are invisible?

Radio waves are all around us, but we can't see them. We use radio waves to send sounds and pictures to radios and televisions. Some radio waves come from satellites in space. A radio set receives radio waves through a metal rod called an aerial. A dish-shaped aerial picks up radio waves for television programmes.

Satellite

Radio waves

Aerial

Radio

Remember

Which part of your body would stop an X-ray? Skin or bone?

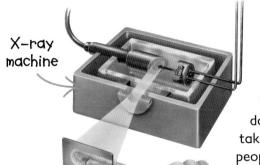
X-ray
machine

Picture
of bone

What is an X-ray?

An X-ray is like a radio wave. X-rays can go through the soft bits of your body. However, hard bones stop them. That's why doctors use X-ray machines to take pictures of the inside of people's bodies.

Space radio!

Radio waves can travel through space. But they can't travel through water. So you can listen to a radio in a space station, but not in a submarine!

Dish-shaped
aerial

What waves can cook food?

Microwaves can. These are a kind of radio wave. They have lots of energy in them. A microwave uses this energy to cook food. Microwaves are fired into the oven. They make the particles in the food jiggle about. This makes the food hot.

Are computers clever?

Not really! Computers are amazing machines, but they can only do what they are told. They carry out computer programs written down by people. These are full of instructions that the computer follows. You can also tell a computer what to do by using its keyboard and mouse.

Typing on a keyboard

Remember

Can you remember the name for a computer's electronic brain? Read these pages again to help you.

Mouse

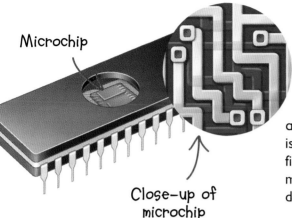

Microchip

Close-up of microchip

Does a computer have a brain?

A computer doesn't have a brain like yours. It has an electronic brain called a central processing unit. This is a microchip the size of your fingernail. This amazing mini machine can do millions of difficult sums in a split second.

Computer

Computer room!

The first computer was made 60 years ago. It was so big that it filled a whole room. A modern calculator can do sums much more quickly!

How does a computer remember?

A computer remembers with its electronic memory. This is made up of lots of tiny microchips. When you turn the computer off, everything in the memory is lost. So you have to save your work on a disc, otherwise you lose it when you switch off.

Is the Internet like a web?

 **The Internet is made up of millions of computers around the world.** They are connected like a giant spider's web! A computer connects to a machine called a modem. This sends signals to a server. The server lets you connect to the Internet. People can send emails and open web pages.

Modem

Email

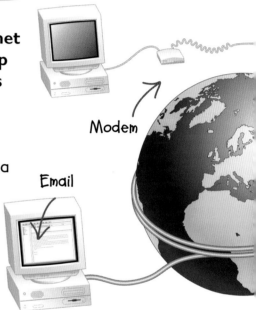

Find out

Look at the main picture on these pages. See if you can find out what the word 'email' is short for.

What does www stand for?

The letters www are short for World Wide Web. The World Wide Web is like a giant library of information, stored on computers all over the world. There are also thousands of shops on the World Wide Web, where you can buy almost anything.

Can I use the Internet without a computer?

Yes. Other machines can link to the Internet, too. You can see simple information from the Internet on a mobile phone. You can send and get emails, too. A mobile phone connects to the Internet by

Server

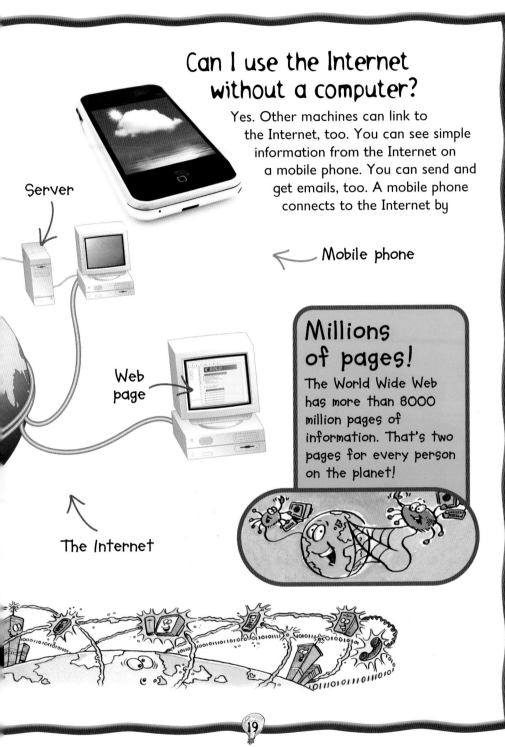

Mobile phone

Web page

The Internet

Millions of pages!

The World Wide Web has more than 8000 million pages of information. That's two pages for every person on the planet!

Can a car be made from card?

Yes, it can – but it would break if you sat inside it! It is always important to use the right material to make something. Cars are made from tough, long-lasting materials. Metal, plastic and rubber are all materials used to make cars.

A racing car is made up of hundreds of parts and different materials

Think

Think of three more materials from which things are made. If you get stuck, ask an adult.

Cotton plants make clothes

What materials grow?

Many of the materials we use every day come from plants. Wood comes from the trunks and branches of trees. Cotton is made from the seeds of cotton plants to make clothes such as T-shirts. Some rubber is made from a liquid (sap) from rubber trees.

Rubber tree makes tyres

Tree trunks and branches make wooden bats

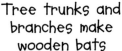

Does glass grow?

Glass doesn't grow! It is made from sand and two other materials called limestone and soda. These materials are mixed together and melted to make a gooey liquid. When the mixture cools down, it forms the hard glass that we use to make windows, drinking glasses and other objects.

Bullet proof!

Some glass is extra-strong. Toughened glass is so hard that even a bullet from a gun bounces off it!

What do scientists do at work?

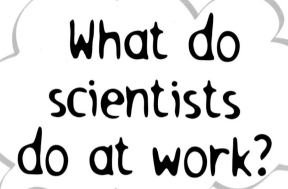

Some scientists try to find out about the world around us. Others find out about space, planets and stars. Some scientists discover useful materials that we can use. Scientists carry out experiments in laboratories to test their ideas.

Scientist in a laboratory

Who is the most famous scientist?

The most famous scientist is called Albert Einstein (1879–1955). He made many discoveries about time, space, the force of gravity and nuclear energy. The ideas that Einstein wrote down were so amazing that they made him famous across the world.

mc^2

Albert Einstein

Atom pie!

One hundred years ago, scientists thought that the pieces in an atom were all spread out, like the raisins in a pudding. Now we know they are all bunched together.

Do scientists help doctors?

Yes, they do. Many scientists make medicines that the doctor gives you when you are ill. They also help to make the complicated machines that doctors use in hospitals. Scientists also try to find out what makes us ill, and how we can stay healthy.

Find

Find out the name of the country where Albert Einstein was born. An encyclopedia will help you.

Index

First published in 2005 by
Miles Kelly Publishing Ltd, Harding's Barr
Bardfield End Green, Thaxted,
Essex, CM6 3PX, UK

Copyright © Miles Kelly Publishing Ltd 20

This edition published 2012

2 4 6 8 10 9 7 5 3 1

Publishing Director Belinda Gallaghe

Creative Director Jo Cowan

Managing Editor Amanda Askew

Volume Designer Elaine Wilkinson

Cover Designer Jo Cowan

Indexer Helen Snaith

Production Manager Elizabeth Collir

Reprographics Stephan Davis,
Lorraine King

Character Cartoonist Mike Foster

ISBN 978-1-84810-894-3

Printed in China

British Library Cataloguing-in-Publication D
A catalogue record for this book is availab
from the British Library

ACKNOWLEDGEMENTS
All artwork from the Miles Kelly Artwork Ba

The publishers would like to thank
XYZ/Shutterstock for the use of the cover
photograph and page 19 Sergej Razvodovsk

All other photographs are from:
Corel, digitalSTOCK, digitalvision, John Foxx
PhotoAlto, PhotoDisc, PhotoEssentials, PhotoP
Stockbyte

Every effort has been made to acknowledge t
source and copyright holder of each picture
Miles Kelly Publishing apologises for any
unintentional errors or omissions.

Made with paper from a sustainable forest

www.mileskelly.net
info@mileskelly.net

www.factsforprojects.com